The Ethiopian Afar & other poems

Antony Fawcus

The Ethiopian Afar
& other poems

The Ethiopian Afar & other poems
ISBN 978 1 76041 004 9
Copyright © Antony Fawcus 2015
Cover photo: Anna Fawcus

First published separately as *Upon Reflection* 2014
and *Time to Stand and Stare* 2012

This edition published 2015 by
GINNINDERRA PRESS
PO Box 3461 Port Adelaide SA 5015
www.ginninderrapress.com.au

Contents

The Ethiopian Afar	9
Abraham	11
The Shadow People	12
The Dancers	13
Corrugated Light	14
The Water Carrier	15
Contagious Laughter	16
The Purple Robe	17
Sickle Magic	18
When Flocks Come Home	19
The Horns of a Dilemma	20
The Woman in Scarlet	21
Children of the Dust	22
The Three Questions	23
Boys of the Afar	24
F.G.C.	25
The Charcoal Burners	26
Other poems	27
The Temptress	29
Summer Heat	30
Drought	31
The Drought Breaks	32
Rain	33
The Currawong	34
Sand Dunes	35
Compromise	36
The Migrant	37
The Angel	38
The Anatomy Student	39
Fear	41

Dreams	42
I Believe	43
Foreclosed Memories	44
The Master of the Hall	45
Old Man Collins	46
Carpe Diem	47
The Paraplegic	49
At the Eleventh Hour	50
Atitlan	51
Puppet on a String	52
The Intellectual	53
The Commuter	54
Yin and Yang	55
Rocks and Stones	56
The Pantoum[14]	57
The Boobook Owl	58
The Elephant Ride	59
Lost for Words	60
To Sappho	61
To Teresa	62
Moth-bound	63
The Sleepy Lizard	64
The Huntsman Spider	65
The Yellow Daffodils	66
Enduring Love	67
St Valentine's Day 2013	68
A Frog He Would A'wooing Go	69
The Three Gifts	70
The Philanderer	71
Oh, What a Bitch!	72
In Memory of My Brother	73
Sudden Death	74

The Poet's End	75
The Cold Hand	76
Winter Solstice	77
For Better or for Worse	78
Life Cycle	79
The Good Man	80
The Eastern Brown Snake	81
Dead Seabirds	82
Transience	83
Dawn (1)	84
Dawn (2)	85
Judgement	86
Cold War	87
On My Niece's First Birthday	88
Assessment	89
Just Do It	90
Remembrance Day	91
The Picnic	92
My First Student	93
Cocktail Party	94
Going to Church	95
Chichén Itzá	96
A Course Critique – for Mem Fox	98
To Jane Covernton (of Omnibus Books)	99
The Hare	100
Migration	101
Wisdom	102
Good and Evil	103
Guilt	104
Bees	105
The Kangaroo	106
Why the Sonnet?	107

Ninja	108
Lemons	109
Nightfall	110
Remains	111
Notes	112

The Ethiopian Afar[1]

Abraham

Who dares divine the thoughts of this dark child
Whose strength derives from Noah's progeny.
With pride he strides across this ancient land
Where warring nomad clans still fight to claw
Subsistence from an unforgiving bowl,
The crucible that forged the birth of man.
Despite a searing sun that burns all hope
His dusky heart belongs to the Afar.[2]

The Shadow People

These are the shadow people,
part of the landscape,
backlit by the fiery glow of dusk
in this,
the hottest place on earth.

They pause awhile to drink
deep draughts of calm
from the cool night that overspills
the bones of this barren land

As beast nuzzles beast
breathing soft silences,
they stand, silhouetted
against an ancient opal sky.

They, like us, are shadows merely
etched in the afterglow of immortality

The Dancers

Three young girls
Were walking home at dusk
With their arms wrapped together
As one

When a sigh in the trees
Rippled through the leaves
And their toes started tapping
In the dust

Their toes started tapping
And itching to the rhythm
The syncopated rhythm
Of their dance

And you couldn't see their feet
As they wove a birdlike flutter
In the utter joyful stutter
Of their dance

Then they swirled and they glided
And they gracefully subsided
In torrents of clear laughter
From their hearts

A taste of the hereafter
The gods have surely given
To those who dance together
In the dust

Corrugated Light

The girl in the red dress
sits in the half-light
facing darkness
but, like all children,
she turns her head
to the light
to follow her dreams
floating free.
Corrugated light falls on this child
as she turns her head
to watch
her dreams floating away.

The Water Carrier

Our water³ comes in bottles;
The corner store's not far,
Just half a mile along the road,
A minute in the car.

Another way to look at it
If on a desert track;
A thousand paces there and then,
A thousand paces back.

Our corner store's the river
With its languid, muddy flow.
It lies beyond the village
And that is where we go

Three times each day we travel
Along the dusty track,
A thousand paces home each time,
Five gallons on the back.

In days gone by, the goatskin,
Though it did not carry wine,
Clung with much more comfort
To the curving of the spine.

Some who carry water
Have a double load to bear,
If they cannot carry both of them
They drop their waters there.

A thousand sorrows wait for those
Who miscarry on the track
But years go by and water is
Still borne upon their back.

Contagious Laughter

This desert daughter flirts with life itself
She brushes worldly woes away like flies
A little imp of mischief parts her lips
And lurks within her lovely laughing eyes

Her laughter spreads contagion like a spark
That sets off smiles in all who linger near
It lights a fire that warms the wand'ring hearts
Of men who seek a love and life to share.

Even in the desert there are flowers
Decked out in colours won from mother earth,
Dyes wrested from her sands and twisted shrubs
To feed our witches' cauldrons of self-worth

We sew them into garments of desire
For they dispel a world of dismal care
They lift our lives from humdrum into dreams
Such magic cloaks can take us anywhere

The Purple Robe

Some say that Sheba[4] ruled this land,
Makeda, mother of the line
Of rightful rulers who held sway
With wisdom steeped in sands of time.
Queen Consort to King Solomon
From whom arose the Axum kings
Who ruled the Ethiopian.

Some say that Moses' Ark is here
That holds the tablets from the mount,
A covenant from God to man
That binds him to the Holy Law,
Secreted by King Menelik
To thwart Manasseh, evil king,
From his ungodly deeds of sin.

Some say this child upon the floor
Is from the ancient line of kings
He has the purple robe and poise
Of thoughtful kingship as he dreams
With inner eye of days to come
But three black flies upon his face
Will bring this boy a gift of myrrh.
They quietly feed upon his face
Around his eyes and running nose
Trachoma,[5] cruel legacy,
Will turn his lashes inward soon
Till sight and dreams will slowly fade
Unless some modern Sheba comes
To bathe his inner eye with balm.

Sickle Magic

This hunters' moon will stain the bones of trees
With shadows steeped in mystic tones of light
Our watchman stands alone, his shape a frieze
Etched harsh above the rising gloom of night,

He points his crescent blade towards the sky
To draw down sickle magic from the moon
Into his wooden club and *jile*[6] held high.
These are his one defence when wild beasts loom

Through rising river mists, and threaten herds
Of camels and uneasy goats, tight-penned
With branches as a last defence, lest words
And sticks and stones and knives cannot defend.

The hunter and the hunted share this land;
The weak will fall, the stronger one will stand.

When Flocks Come Home

A rondeau

When flocks come home beneath a haze
Of dust caught in the sun's last rays,
Their cloven hooves create a sound
That picks up pace now homeward bound
To safe corrals and husks of maize.

Though thorny scrub gives leaves to graze
It has been sparse through drought-dead days
So girls will spread these husks around
When flocks come home.

Such girls the men will soon appraise,
For beauty better bride-wealth pays
In precious goats. This will redound
With credit on the goddess found
With hennaed hair and hip that sways
When flocks come home.

The Horns of a Dilemma

A sonnet

The coffee's grown for you and me to sup,
We stir in sugar for a sweeter taste,
Our hearts beat faster, and it revs us up
To self-destruct with more frenetic haste.

Such mono-cultures swiftly have displaced
The crops on which these people so depend
For life. Our sprays leave naught but toxic waste
To satisfy the caffè latte trend.

We chatter on about the perfect blend
Of coffee, not of life for those who sweat
For cash to buy the food they ought to tend.
Such money does not grow on trees, and yet

They feed our foibles for this phantom wealth
Instead of planting crops for their own health.[7]

The Woman in Scarlet

'We may be surprised at the people we find in heaven. God has a soft spot for sinners. His standards are quite low.' – Archbishop Desmond Tutu

Poor sinners wear the scarlet cloak.
Was it ever thus?

She gave her body
and her blood
that others might live,
and she was adored.

Christ lives in her,
poor sinner that she is.

Even the Magi who knelt
to adore the Christ Child
wore scarlet robes.

They too had travelled far.

Children of the Dust

A counting rhyme

One can see them,
only two, only just,
from afar.

These children
of the dust
roaming free

are getting hard to see.

The girl might be three
Or maybe four
But not much more

For a third don't survive
To five
in the Afar.[8]

The Three Questions

inspired by an Ethiopian folk tale from the Afar

What is this dream, my desert child, that shapes your lovely smile?
Why do you bend your magic wand? What prince will you beguile?
The dream I dream is of a man whose load is hard to bear.
What is this load, my tender love, that bends him down with care?
Is it the stone upon his back that grinds him to the earth?
Nay, replied the loving child, it's the giving of his oath.

Indeed there's childhood magic in this wand that slices air
What else my child, my tender child, does fill your dreams with care?
My dream is of the sweetest food, the sweetest food of all.
What is this food, my tender love, that makes all others pall?
Is it the sweetness of the bees that hover round the hive?
Not so! It is the food that keeps a starving man alive.

The magic in this pliant wand lets precious dreams fly free,
There is one deeper dream I think that fills your reverie.
I dream the sweetest smell on earth will fill my life with love
What is this scent, my tender child, that you are dreaming of?
Is it the smell of rosemary, reminder of the dead?
Nay! It's the scent of innocence breathed from my baby's head.

Boys of the Afar

We give our children toys to play at war.[9]
These ones are not mere toys, they are their life
They stalk their foes and with their guns they shoot
To kill wild beasts and wild marauding men
Who come to steal their precious flock of goats
The tribal wealth, the sum of all they own
These two young guards will keep the village safe
Then laugh and play with sticks when they come home.

F.G.C.

Asunder, sad Afar, a girl adrift
Bonds of marriage planned and circumcision
Such traumatic custom, a tragic rift
That kisses death with each cruel incision[10]

Two centimetres more Dabbahu slips
Weeping the warm pulse of labial lips
Deep into the Danakil Depression[11]
An ancient lore, an obscene oppression

The Charcoal Burners

The leaves just whispered when the night winds came
To drive the ragged clouds across the sky
Like refugees escaping certain doom.
My tree, alas, was rooted deep and held
Its silver minnows swishing to break free,
Their sighing scales a softly spoken dirge
Prescient of the axeman's ringing blows.

The moon climbed like a pallid elfin child
That scaled the ancient lemon-scented limbs
To blush their mottled nakedness with rue.
Sad angels shed their tears across the sky,
Gold sequins in the counterpane of night,
Sewn one by one to mark each tree that died,
Rough-hewn, clear felled, to fill the charcoal kiln.[12]

The silent, sweating men have dragged their loads
Barefoot across the arid desert sands
For man's insatiable demand for fire.
Demented inward circles piled up high,
Each circle stacked with scarce a vent for breath,
Foreshadow hell with smouldering intent,
As hell must surely follow such dark work.

The kiln is now a smoking charnel heap,
Its suffocating mound a funeral pyre
Infused with thick and sweet incense of death
That seeps into the muddy Awash flow
Where crocodiles shed tears for trees cut down,
So sadly matched by weeping of our own.
I listen to my tree and hear it moan.

Other poems

The Temptress

I lay under the stars, scanning the universe
for signs of a kindred spirit swirling through space
in concentric circles around my soul.
How distant my dreams,
how filled with despair
of ever capturing a wandering star
within my orbit, dragging her down
into the black hole of my being,
but that night one fell
from the serpent bearer's belt.
Slithering through the sands
of time she came,
her flickering tongue
sensing my desire
as she slid along my nakedness,
so vulnerable to her rainbow wiles.
I prayed that she might strike swiftly,
congealing my heart's blood.
How tempting to go that way
on this, the eve of my life.

Summer Heat

Forty degrees, and every leaf is still.
Gaunt skeletons of opium poppies
have spread black seed beneath saffron thistles
and tangled mess of drought-defying weeds.
Convolvulus climbs the Christmas lilies
and bindweed strangles the green-eyed hellebore.
In this mesmeric haze of summer heat
it seems the gardener too has wilted.

Drought

Saltbush-encrusted subsistence
Where the life that measures rainfall
Measures the depth of tears
That fall on arid lands
Cracked earth
Weeping
Scarce enough
Dried-up emotion
To sustain another season

The Drought Breaks

Our golden elm begins to lose its leaves
Now autumn comes. The hillsides turn to green
With long-awaited rain and cattle, lean
Through summer drought, will graze beyond the trees
Where they have sheltered patiently at ease
And waited. What a wait this year it's been.
Jessie we lost and our best milker, Jean.
The day we buried her there was no breeze
To cool our sweat-drenched backs and dry the tears
Of our daughter, who mourned this closest friend
With whom she shared her secret hopes and fears.
In time perhaps her heartfelt hurt will mend;
In time. Though with the passing of the years
She'll find that love has further wounds to lend.

Rain

Raindrops on rooftops, flowing down gutters
Into the tanks with splashing and splutters,
Cascading down creeks and into the dams
Saving the lives of our sheep and our lambs

For this we have yearned throughout the long dry
Praying for rainfall before they all die
Five seasons of drought have parched the dry earth
Now we're collecting for all we are worth!

The Currawong

For a moment the world stands still;
The sheoak has ceased her whispering.
A currawong, sharp silhouette
Against the opalescent sky,
Sings the sun down softly
Here in Ratalang, at Sandy Bay.
Her gentle warbling ascends to soothe
The spirit ancestors that guard this land
And me.

Sand Dunes

Not much grows at the leading edge of dunes;
They bear the brunt of the seas that mould them.
Trailing grasses sprawl down the sheltered side
Solidifying shape for low grey scrub,
Toehold territory for sand dune shrubs,
Shade and safety for a sleepy lizard
And a haven for swift small birds, darting
Transient, to and fro and twittering
At a sinuous track in the warm soft sand.
A snake lies hidden in this paradise,
Coiled around a cache of broken shells and dreams,
Shattered by the thunderous foaming roar
Of life, and the relentless tides of time.

Compromise

I started this morning to speak with my daughter.
We sat in silence in the sunshine,
Preliminaries subsumed in silence.
I had wanted of course to ask what troubled her
But could not find the words.
In the end, she took the initiative
And told me what troubled me
Gently goading the artist and writer
Submerged not far below the surface
Of my bread and butter life.
She knew with the unencrusted wisdom of youth
What I chose to forget:
Self-fulfilment is an uncompromising venture.

Unlike her, I have taken the dripping poison of time
And it has taught me fear,
A most invidious addiction,
Yet I live the lie that it is under control.
Drugs provide an illusion of life enhanced
Sharply in contrast with commonplace realities,
But in so doing
They widen a gulf of depression and hopelessness.
The compromises of age do much the same
Only more slowly.

The Migrant

There is a part of me I did not bring
To this new land I choose to call my own.
Even the migrant bird returns in spring.
I find my heart is only here on loan

When harebells ring across the Chiltern Hills
With skylark songs that woo the chalk blue sky.
Beech trees dapple a bluebell wood that fills
My childhood dreams. It's then I wonder why

I chose this ancient land. Her limbs are gaunt
And bare against the glare of scorching sun
Which turns the earth to ochre bones that haunt
Much older dreams than those I had begun.

My dream now soars in starlit southern skies
And homeless here shall hang until it dies.

The Angel

An angel came down to help me,
To assuage my sorrow she came
So my life could go on again,
But through the tears I could not see
Who she was that comforted me.
I felt the breathe that eased my pain;
It bathed my soul like gentle rain
And bore my grief far out to sea.
An aching heart now takes its place;
I long to draw the veil aside
And see heaven light up her face,
But this alas must be denied
Until I reach a state of grace
And I, too, cross the great divide.

The Anatomy Student

A gust came first, of fetid air like death,
Then tortured metal forced the Tube to pause
At ten past nine. The doors rolled back agape
As they disgorged their rush-hour remnant few
With such a languid yawn and hollow groan
As sank the hearts of those whose lot it was
To meet their Waterloo this winter morn
On Platform Two.
                He pulled his collar up
And stamped his feet for warmth as he exhaled
A misty stream of breath that drifted up
Into the girder grid of netted glass
And died beneath the station clock, where clung
An icy amputee that dripped its life
Away into the slush and grime below.

Then, with a sudden turn of speed he strode,
Head down, towards the busy London street
That led him to the portals of Saint Luke,
Where dead men teach the living how to hone
The scalpel sharpness of their mind and eye.

Within, he climbed the winding marble stair
Whose wrought-iron balustrade led ever up
To the dissection room. He was unnerved.
Each alcove held a silent row of jars,
Each one with organs drowned in fluid crypts;
The livers, testes, tumours, broken hearts
Of those beyond the surgeon's blunted knife;
Pale textbook trophies wrested from the dead.

Nine foetuses were graded month by month,
To make a silent guard of sentinels
That stood in pre-birth wisdom in a row
To mark his entry to the fourth floor lab.
The door swung shut and caused a whispered breeze
That caught and slightly swayed a set of bones
That hung and seemed a living skeleton
To lead the serried ranks of those who served.

Formaldehyde, a pungent creeping ghost,
Both blurred his eyes and clutched his nose and throat.
Unsteadily he swam across the room
Towards a window seat, and there below
He watched cadavers queue to board the bus
To Bethnal Green. The room began to fill.
He took his book and leant it on a limb.
Page One. Incision One. His term began.

Fear

Last night I trod a field of childhood dreams,
Across a brook where leaves were barques of gold.
Each shiny pebble glinting in the sun
Was treasure found to strain my pocket seams.
I felt a shiver, not delight but cold,
Then shrugged and ran across the grass for fun
And started up a hare beneath my feet
So sudden that my heart near stopped its beat.

I still remember that lost pulse of life,
The hare that zigged and zagged across the park,
A blur of brown amid the fescue green
That cut a swaying swath away from strife.
Then all was still again but one lone lark,
A distant speck of song above the scene.
I witnessed fear that day and felt it too,
A cloud had smudged my sky of harebell blue.

Dreams

This night
I shall course through cold rocks
and follow quartz seams
to the dull gleam
of thoughts
hidden within.

I shall lie in Arcadian woods
buried in cool loam
amongst bluebells.

I shall ride the warm breath
of the night sea
and sing to selkies
sealing my fate.

I shall curl in the helix of shells
among the ingrained sands of my being
and dream.

I Believe

We humans have a deeply felt desire
To shift the blame onto someone higher
So we have religions sent from above
With diverse gods to plant the seeds of love.

Then clever men created better gods
To wield their power over rotten sods
Like us; thus to preserve the status quo
That favoured them, the people in the know.

New people wanting power make new schisms.
So now we have innumerable isms.
Their greed for power has caused unending strife
Loss of liberty, cruel waste of life.

Yet each says that his god is there for good
Acting as a light to show how we should
Behave towards each other. Yet they vie
On points of difference and for those we die.

But the central point, that in their blindness
They miss, is that all are based on kindness.
When I see an act of love, I see God.
When I perform it, I am He – that's odd.

Man-made religions often hide this fact;
You build your own god through your every act.

Foreclosed Memories

Do the birds still sing?
Can you see the small things;
Taste the wine?
Tell me,
For I still feel with my heart,
Not clumsily
As with my hands.

What was that you said?

Shadows walk with me
In the night
Of people I have known,
My generation all
Are faded
Album photographs
I no longer see.

Take heed
Before you, too, become
A foreclosed memory.

The Master of the Hall

'I am Graf von Glehn;
Master of this Hall!'
A dying echo
haunts the castle wall.

A black swan whoops
from the ice's edge;
her answer fades
in the whispering sedge.

Moonlight creeps
up the smooth grey stone
where my lord lies shadowed
in grief, alone.

The white peacock struts,
tail spread like lace,
mocking the frosted boughs,
and his lord's disgrace.

Old Man Collins

a picture by Hans Heysen

Youth strides out across the canvas,
Eager to start on life's journey,
Keen to get to the other side.

He pauses midway, impeded,
And lights his clay pipe to ponder
The ghost of himself, old Collins,
In no hurry to leave the picture.

Carpe Diem

I met a man upon life's dusty road.
His head was bowed; a dog was at his heel.
Upon his back a bag, wherein was stowed
His worldly goods and pan of pitted steel
In which, God grant, to cook his daily meal
Providing providence and cunning wiles
Enabled him to beg, or maybe steal,
To staunch his hunger, gird him for his trials
And give him strength again to tread tomorrow's miles.

I spoke with him and nodded to his cur
And asked him how much further we must tread
To reach our goal. His answer was a slur
Of words from which I guessed that more than bread
Had passed his lips that day and that his head
Was fuddled with some diabolic brew,
But I was wrong, for he looked up and said
Some words so clear they struck me straight and true:
'The way may be long, my friend, but the sky is blue.'

I had not thought it so when I left home
That day and closed the door upon my life
Of comfort, again to search, to roam
The world, engage once more in petty strife
Turn the grindstone with which to whet the knife
That cuts through want and garners fruits of ease,
But at what ghastly price? What ghastly price?
Our constant search for future wealth, like bees,
May fill tomorrow's store but is today's disease.

The dog concurred with a wag of his tail,
For dogs are happy with what they have got,
Unlike their masters, who quite often fail
To enjoy life now, content with their lot,
Their noses to the ground where the scent is hot,
Taking joy in the chase, not in the prize,
Which will elude them as often as not.
I think that if dogs could only advise,
They'd bark, 'Pluck the day, before your demise!'

The Paraplegic

He enlisted at sixteen,
trained for a few months
and was sent to the trenches.
His war lasted less than a day.

When the order came to attack
he was hit by friendly fire
from behind.

I saw him, fifty years later
In a sunny corner of the ward,
studying the racing pages
from the comfort of his wheelchair.
Against all the odds,
he had eventually become good
at picking a winner.

At the Eleventh Hour

I count my years in jacaranda days
at this unleavened hour of dust and ash.
A ragged regiment of ancient trees
drank deep in hidden springs of indigo
to stain these bugle blooms that post our dead
in gutter drifts, the purple prose of war.
They fall as gentle as an angel's wing
upon the plain grey pavement of my heart
reminding me of those who gave their lives
while we, the war-torn residue, now stand
in ranks and feel the unbecoming calm
of this fine day, a mask to hide the deaths
of these, our mates we fought with side by side.

Atitlan

I had in mind to write of Atitlan's
Volcanic peaks and depths, unplumbed as yet;
Her mirrored calm shimmering at sunset;
The breathless beauty of the sacred toucan
That goes between the spirit world and man
Protecting him from evils that beset
The simple souls who daily cast their net;
Fishermen surviving as best they can.

But one small boy, Ernesto, fills my eye.
Ernesto, tin box like a carapace,
Cries 'Shoeshine!' each day in desperate sweat
For patrons who have a quetzal to buy
A shoeshine mirror of his earnest face,
To ease the burden of his family's debt.

Puppet on a String

A nonet

The puppeteer makes her dance his tune,
Pulling her strings this way and that
Not heeding her heartfelt pleas.
While forcing her to bend
He pretends that she's
His mere plaything;
Which is rot.
She is
Not.

The Intellectual

Pale gormless fish
Swim endlessly in circles
Round Heshbon's[13] pools
Mirroring a madness
Carved from the years.

Step by step
I climbed the tower
That now imprisons me.

As I look down
On the world below
No longer part of it,
My mind encircles
Knowledge
Endlessly
But cannot break in,
Cannot break out
Of my ivory tower.

From here
The problems of the world
Seem small.

Imprisoned in an ivory tower,
Unless a god,
One is merely
Another dead elephant
In the room.

The Commuter

Huddled against the wind and rain
With eyes cast down on pavements grey
Hope crushed, like blossom torn away
From trees, I hurried for my train.
Reflected in those slabs, with pain
I feared my footprint lost that day,
Trapped with the leaden skies that lay
Fractured within each flagstone's stain.

Then, looking up, I found a land
Of spires, sun-drenched and shining gold,
Framed by towering banks of cloud,
God's backdrop to man's outstretched hand,
And was refreshed, once more made bold
To seek my way through life's dark shroud.

Yin and Yang

The eternal circle ensnares a snake
Whose sinuous form marks the division
Between death and life. Too soon we will take
That fatal step, out of this world's frission.

But while there is life there's a game to play.
It's a lover's glance; it's a game of chance.
It is happening now, so seize the day.
Whirl while you may, with the Lord of the Dance!

For all bets are off when the circle spins.
Fear the racking cough of the silver ball
Ere it comes to rest and the devil grins.
If it drops in zero, he scoops up all
Except for the memories. They remain
To enhance the play of the next man's game.

Rocks and Stones

This glass jar's full of rocks and stones,
The sum of all the old man owns,
Fragments and shards of life gone by,
Whose sharp edges and muted tones

Mean nothing to another's eye.
There's Machu Picchu's Inca dye
On that one, where he met Suzanne
The girl he wooed and then stood by

For all those years, until the scan
That showed the cancer that began
To eat away her life; his all.
That concrete tells where he outran

The guards and scaled the Berlin Wall,
Then turned to help free Friedrich Kohl,
His friend ensnared by razor wire,
Whose cruel barbs held him in thrall.

'What have we here?' nurses enquire.
'A few worthless rocks in a jar?
No precious stones with inner fire?'
'Look deeper, nurse! You'll find there are.'

The Pantoum[14]

All hail, Pantoum, Malay malaise
Pan pipes entomb a dual sense
Tucked up within each other's phrase
With treasure shared beyond expense

Pan pipes entomb a dual sense
Lines fixed in one climb up a rung
With treasure shared beyond expense
A pantomime so richly sung

Lines fixed in one climb up a rung
As sense now slides across the verse
A pantomime so richly sung
Takes time and causes one to curse

As sense now slides across the verse
At last the tail engulfs the head
Takes time and causes one to curse
So here's an end. It's put to bed

At last the tail engulfs the head
Tucked up within each other's phrase
So here's an end. It's put to bed
All hail, Pantoum, Malay malaise

The Boobook Owl

A pantoum

The Boobook owl kills silently,
her shadowed silver silhouette
suggested in the ghost gum tree,
her whisper close to flight and yet

her shadowed silver silhouette
stays poised. She looks for swaying sedge,
her whisper close to flight and yet
her prey, alert at water's edge,

stays poised. She looks for swaying sedge
reflected by the hunter's moon.
Her prey, alert at water's edge,
will make her fateful movement soon,

reflected by the hunter's moon.
A wraith with hooded orange eye
will make her fateful movement soon,
her talons piercing death's small cry!

A wraith with hooded orange eye
suggested in the ghost gum tree,
her talons piercing death's small cry,
the boobook owl kills silently.

The Elephant Ride

A pantoum

The elephant sways side to side
Seeking solace from her despair
At what dire cost our tourist ride
How dastardly[15] her journey here

Seeking solace from her despair
She treads the path that crushed[16] her dreams
How dastardly her journey here
This tourist ride her life demeans

She treads the path that crushed her dreams
Ganesh the god must shed a tear
This tourist ride her life demeans
Her wistful eye so full of fear

Ganesh the god must shed a tear
At what dire cost our tourist ride
Her wistful eye so full of fear
The elephant sways side to side

Lost for Words

A pantoum

My tongue now stumbles over words
They disassemble in my brain
They fluster like a flock of birds
Unravel what I've said again

They disassemble in my brain
My mind is blank, the words dispersed
Unravel what I've said again
I grasp for meanings now reversed

My mind is blank, the words dispersed
Like ancient leaves that fall from trees
I grasp for meanings now reversed
They slip and swirl and gently tease

Like ancient leaves that fall from trees
My thoughts are lost. They're not my own
They slip and swirl and gently tease
My mind's a shell I have outgrown

My thoughts are lost. They're not my own
They fluster like a flock of birds
My mind's a shell I have outgrown
My tongue now stumbles over words

To Sappho

A pantoum

Aboard my silent silver ship
I sped. The wind was in my soul
I set out on a lonely trip
The isle of Lesbos was my goal

I sped. The wind was in my soul
A nightmare journey though it seems
The isle of Lesbos was my goal
To find my Sapphic cave of dreams

A nightmare journey though it seems
Cruel Eros made it hard for me
To find my Sapphic cave of dreams
He set my heart adrift at sea

Cruel Eros made it hard for me
To sing my soul's eternal tune
He set my heart adrift at sea
My lyric voice beseeched the moon

To sing my soul's eternal tune
With notes of tidal lunacy
My lyric voice beseeched the moon
Will Sappho ever join with me

With notes of tidal lunacy
I set out on a lonely trip
Will Sappho ever join with me
Aboard my silent silver ship

To Teresa

A 19th century villanelle

Teresa's gown of Tuscan lace
Is set with iridescent pearls
That vie in vain with her fresh face

She holds herself with simple grace
And all admire her as she swirls
Teresa's gown of Tuscan lace

Dares lift her bust with close embrace
I see the eyes of dukes and earls
That vie in vain for her fresh face

They spur my heart to kick the trace
And boldly dream that it unfurls
Teresa's gown of Tuscan lace

To hold her gentle in its place
The dreams of love that Cupid hurls
That vie in vain with her fresh face

Have killed my lust for other girls
My one desire is to displace
Teresa's gown of Tuscan lace
And lay my claim to her fresh face

Moth-bound

A villanelle

This is my soul that's pressed against the sky.
It yearns to tear the veils from misted dreams
To find itself, not flimsy moths that fly

And are consumed in reason's fiery eye.
Reader, be kind, for this isn't what it seems,
This is my soul that's pressed against the sky

And if you feel it not, my pen is dry.
My muse will drag me down in sorrow's streams
To find itself, not flimsy moths that fly

Against the worldly flames where they must die
In withered ash of countless wasted reams.
This is my soul that's pressed against the sky.

It seeks the truth. Don't mock it with the lie
Of vacant prose. It braves the solar beams
To find itself, not flimsy moths that fly

In darkness searching for a light that gleams
Below. Not there, I tell them with a sigh!
This is my soul that's pressed against the sky
To find itself, not flimsy moths that fly.

The Sleepy Lizard

A villanelle

This sleepy lizard is my garden friend
Nature has given him a good defence
You'd think he had a head at either end

One is a fake but good enough to lend
His foes a puzzled look at this pretence
This sleepy lizard is my garden friend

He eats the hornèd snails before they send
Me into righteous rage and make me tense
You'd think he had a head at either end

When he is challenged he can just pretend
It is bad breath if by mischance he vents
This sleepy lizard is my garden friend

His bottom with his face does neatly blend
Not handsome but he does not take offence
You'd think he had a head at either end

The way those slimy gastropods distend
His frame. He really gets immense!
This sleepy lizard is my garden friend
You'd think he had a head at either end

The Huntsman Spider

A villanelle

Oh God! It's in the bathroom! Kill it, dear!
A Huntsman spider clung against the wall
What murder we commit because of fear

I took the can and sprayed its derrière
It quivered, lost its grip and had to fall
Oh God! It's in the bathroom! Kill it, dear!

The can says instant death to bugs, right here!
It was not instant death though. Not at all!
What murder we commit because of fear

It crawled until it could no longer bear
Its bulbous body weight, so full of gall
Oh God! It's in the bathroom! Kill it, dear!

At length its legs curled underneath its rear
I sadly took the corpse down through the hall
What murder we commit because of fear

I pray that when my time for death draws near
His Wife does not give Him a panic call
Oh God! It's in the bathroom! Kill it, dear!
What murder we commit because of fear

The Yellow Daffodils

A terzanelle

The yellow daffodils
Now trumpet in the spring,
The yellow daffodils

Now start their strumpeting,
Their pretty pouting lips
Now trumpet in the spring.

They sway a wild ellipse
As wanton winds do press
Their pretty pouting lips

And shamelessly possess
Each joyful yellow bloom.
As wanton winds do press

Their suit with warm perfume
Some fickle gusts will tease
Each joyful yellow bloom

With laughter, as they seize
The yellow daffodils.
Some fickle gusts will tease
The yellow daffodils.

Enduring Love

Soft spoken whispers in the wind
still sigh amongst the fever trees
and haunt the tropic tamarind
awaking distant memories
of velvet nights when we did moan
in languid love on moonlit shores.
For though such moments now are flown,
my heart stays true and still adores
that nymph whose lips impressed my mind.
Now flotsam on life's eventide,
we surf the smaller swells we find
and drift together, side by side,
until by death's dread storm at last
upon another strand we're cast.

St Valentine's Day 2013

We wrote in Tolkien's strange language
When we started out together.
Letters began, '*Mi querida*'.
Wedding bells rang at Rose Cottage;
Justice was done at the marriage.
We walked through life in all weather
Wearing it light as a feather
When it was filled with less baggage.

Thirty-five years loving each other
And, though I seldom express it,
There lies, buried deep in my heart,
A love that life cannot smother.
Words, in themselves, do not say it,
But nothing can tear us apart.

A Frog He Would A'wooing Go

Knee deep in diamonds
Walking through the dew
Knee deep in diamonds
Deep in love with you

As droplets capture sunshine
Upon each grassy stalk
Your eyes reflect the sunshine
Every time we talk

Clouds that block the sun above
Are merely passing through
Tears of life are tears of love
When they're shared with you

You swept away my sadness
Replaced it with the sun
My tears are now of gladness
Now we go through life as one.

Knee deep in diamonds
Walking through the dew
Knee deep in diamonds
Deep in love with you

The Three Gifts

The gift I gave of finest lace
Set off the beauty of her face.
I gave it her with all good grace.

My love I gave to her also.
She took it, kept it; it did grow
Until she found another beau.

I swore revenge without remit
And she discovered bit by bit,
When I give my word, I keep it.

The Philanderer

A rondeau

All beauty pales when set by Sue,
A diamond in a drop of dew,
A rainbow held inside a pearl,
The petal morning mists unfurl,
But all of these I shall eschew

And for a week I shall be true
To darling Sue, and then we're through,
For though she is the sweetest girl
All beauty pales

When it's despoiled. So long! Adieu!
I shall be off to hunt anew
And maybe find a chorus girl.
My life shall be a giddy whirl
Until I'm old, then – déjà vu –
All beauty pales.

Oh, What a Bitch!

A rondeau

'Oh, what a bitch! Oh, what a tail!'
He thought, while sniffing her in braille
He woof-whistled, his tongue hung out,
This was no time to mess about.
He slipped his leash and reached the grail

And mounted her. He did assail
Her nether end. A force 9 gale!
And then her mistress yanked her snout.
Oh, what a bitch!

Not so! My heart did almost fail.
A princess from a fairy tale
She surely was. I asked her out.
She mouthed disdain with horrid pout
And my hopes felt the coffin nail.
Oh, what a bitch!

In Memory of My Brother

Death paused, but passed me by this day,
Upon another errand bent.
We knew the reason he'd been sent.
He hovered where my brother lay.
'There's no hurry,' I heard him say
As through his rattling chest he went,
Deep into bones with grim intent.
We begged – but he was here to stay.

I wished it me he'd come to take,
Instead of dismembering him
As he lay in a morphine sleep.
We grieve. We grieve for Simon's sake
As we offer up an ancient hymn
Of thanks for memories we keep.

Sudden Death

Silences lack sound not meaning
They come still in the night
Unblinking
With the owl's orange hooded eye
Steady, with penetrated meaning
Then swooping on the wing of the night
With quiet fury
Talons tear.
The heart's blood falls
In a wide and darkening pool
Staining the soul with an ebbing warmth
That once took the name of love.
Only the moon hears the wind whispers
Only the moon heard that final silent cry
Only the moon.

The Poet's End

A spot of red.
A haemorrhoidal stain
he thought,
from too much sitting
writing piles of verse,
or perhaps
just sodding retribution
for time misspent with youth.

But no,
this time it was death
came oozing out.
A messy end for one
normally so
anally retentive.

The Cold Hand

Today
I felt
the cold hand
of my doctor
on my heart.

Winter Solstice

He hung himself at night alone on Bushey Heath
With old school ties knotted, rather than face the shame.
His body swung limp, eerie in the glow of dawn,
A diadem of dew crowned dark bedraggled hair
As sunrise sidled across his blank staring face;
A lifeless form slowly spinning. He cut the thread
Himself, not trusting Atropos, the hand of fate.
Tears his friends wept dropped in the icy pool of death
And each one that fell spread circles of emptiness
On the muddy water of that midwinter night.

For Better or for Worse

For better or for worse,
Bonded by mutual indifference,
Mutual utility
And occasional friendship,

For forty years
They breakfasted together, almost.
Each night they returned,
Richer or poorer,

Bored each other
With meaningless transactions
And watched TV
Till death did them part.

Life Cycle

There is a millennium of miles
Between each fiery circle
Contiguously purchasing
The miracle of life
With death.

The short sweet blooming
Is scented and blushes
As lovers do.
Petals fall like tears
Soft fruits swell
Luscious
Lascivious
Fomenting birth.

A small myth
A mystery
Lies dormant
Till its time is come

That deep down thing
We did mistake for death
Is only dormancy.

The Good Man

He willed his final resting place to be
The village churchyard with its ancient yew
Where wood pigeons roost and gently coo
Their warbled cadences from tree to tree.
A place to lie in peace, at last set free.
Now dragonflies hover, gossamer blue,
Like elfin spirits, darting fro and to,
Above the stone that holds his memory,

He who wasted life, threescore years and ten,
A life of lies hidden between the lines;
Born 1828, belov'd…now dead.
Time has erased his intervening crimes
Committed in the name of God on men.
Life's dragonflies have less to leave unsaid.

The Eastern Brown Snake

A rispetto

Unseen on logs inside the shed,
The coils of copper blurred as he
Up-reared and hissed with flattened head,
His startled eye fixed straight on me.

Heart stopped for Death to change its mind.
Upon this day the fates were kind,
He slithered down behind a bale
And spared my life. I tell the tale.

Dead Seabirds

A quatern

Dead seabirds cast upon the shore
Did overreach themselves like words
Poets set down in rhythmic waves,
To gradually decompose,

Clawed from the air where once they flew.
Dead seabirds cast upon the shore
Floating, listless, aloft no more,
Then thrown up by the gaping maw

Of an incoming tide, flotsam
Rejected by the restless sea.
Dead seabirds cast upon the shore,
Their weed-strewn sentence scrawled in sand,

A lonely place where poets come
To capture moonlit silver pools,
But find their verses often are
Dead seabirds cast upon the shore.

Transience

(In memory of Stefan Heysen)

I heard last week that Stefan passed away.
He held this land for nigh on fifty year.
Memories he shaped crop up everywhere
Imprinted on the place and to this day,
Ten years on, come sunshine or sea-mist grey,
His spirit whispers yet in Brooklands' air.
Old tools rust where he lost them, here and there
By fences. Good tools once, I hear him say.

Since taking the stewardship from his hand
I have dug out weeds, rebuilt and mended;
Transient efforts to repair a past
That lies so recent on this ancient land.
Despite the effort we've both expended,
Ngurunderi will claim it back at last.

Dawn (1)

I lay alone upon the beach, listening for the dawn.
A soft wind came,
Scarce breath enough to sway the palms,
Caressed the sea and passed along the shore.
All was quiet
But for the lapping of waves tugging at the strand,
Sleeplessly insistent,
Too soft a murmur to fright the sidling crab
Creeping from his hole with scoops of sand
Then scuttling back lest the world should see
The fear within his stalk-held eyes.
A dog barked. Two birds swept low across the water,
Then a burnished brightness over-spilled the ocean's edge
Flooding a molten path across the sea
And the crab turned and faced the dawn
Defiant – and for a single instant primevally brave.

Dawn (2)

Dawn caresses the restless sea,
Tugs gently at a stooping palm,
Murmurs soft the morning psalm,
But wakens not the shadowy tree.

Each ripple breasts the coral strand,
Surging ashore with puny crash,
Then recedes to yield its cache
Of watery shells and time-worn sand.

Timelessness fills the morning air
And whispers soft of latent power.
A crab creeps from his ivory tower,
Stops – then scuttles back in fear.

Judgement

I claw the darkness, rend the folds of night,
Ascending from the pit upon a wing,
The gift of unknown gods that keep my soul
Unbroken by the blows of fate, and free
From the iron jaw of bloody circumstance.
Released, I stand before my final judge
Uncompromised, prepared to tell my years,
For I have spun no webs, no gossamer
Of lies to bind me down at last in death.

Cold War

A balance of arms is a balance of power,
Is the balance of life in the fateful hour.
A balance of mind is the balance of all.
If that should fail, then all must fall.
The balance of fate in the hands of the few
Is a fateful balance for me and you,
For power can tip the balance of mind
And blow off the limbs of all mankind,
Blow out the candle of every life
And extinguish this world in nuclear strife.

On My Niece's First Birthday

Miss Alison Kate is one, tra la!
Miss Alison Kate is one.

Her life has just begun, tra la!
Her life has just begun.

Let's give a rousing cheer, tra la!
For this new Australian bear, tra la!

To Alison Kate,
The toast of the State,
My very best mate
Miss Alison Kate

And a slice of her birthday cake, tra la!
And a slice of her birthday cake.

Assessment

Pray for a Grade A, praise and free graze;
Defrayed gold; gilt.
Become prey to a grey day; gaze and freeze.
Cold rays defrayed; guilt.
Faint praise enfolded grows gross;
Retailed – grosser.
Feint!
Erase nightmares once foaled.
Friesians graze in the sun's rays.
True praise!
Happy days!

Just Do It

Climb before your heart grows cold,
Impelled by your own insistence.
Attempt the hill!
It's worth being bold
For losses grow larger with distance.

Remembrance Day

Is it Remembrance Day once more, and well
To honour them? Inside the Albert Hall
Petals to represent the brave souls fall
Gently – unlike the screaming men who fell
In war, when words were not enough to quell
The rising power and armour-plated gall
Of monstrous tyrants. Now, once more, a wall
Of rhetoric cradles a newborn hell.
I smelt charnel fires lingering in the scent
Of a speech last summer. For it was said
More than a million dollars are now spent
Each minute on defence. The monster's fed.
After this madness we shall need to be lent
More than a minute to honour our dead.

The Picnic

It had been a long walk to this place by the water's edge
Down a path through the pine woods,
Even though there were wild raspberries along the way
And the sun shone on gossamer'd bracken.

It was end-of-July hot
Swarmed with iridescent flies
And midges hanging in the still air;
But a light wind at the water's edge
Cooled a place to feed our child
Secretly hidden
In a rooted outcrop of young oak trees.

We stopped there,
Covered the ground with grandfather's travelling rug
And suckled the child
While small birds squabbled discordantly
For seeds in the tall grasses.

Oak leaves quicken to the summer breeze,
A soft elfin wind dances
Quicksilver on the rippling wave
And our child
Contentedly chuckles on grandfather's rug
Chasing midsummer sunbeams
At this place by the water's edge.

My First Student

She is an unkempt girl with a wild eye,
Her huge mouth's trusting grin seeks approval,
Her wide brown eyes stare, quizzically crossed,
Pleading – the way a dog used to beatings
Cringes on its belly, wagging its tail,
Ingratiating, then widdles on the floor
Inviting another kick or beating –
A harsh word – or any form of notice.

Cocktail Party

The stuffed-shirt hovers, afraid of the birds
That parade in silks as flimsy as words.
They preen and smooth their shimmering dresses
As, twittering on, they exchange addresses.
He samples the board: larks' tongues, stuffed eggs.
More gins and lime, then…oh! Those heavenly legs!
They capture his senses as she comes to his side
But her wiles are wasted! He's ostrich-eyed.

Going to Church

We are an upright family in full sail,
Steering a quiet course to eternity
Down the charnel path to prayer.

Beside this path lies a rolling sea of graves,
Drunken memorials proclaiming the virtues
Of a silent host of unfulfilled dreams.

We pity these dead men who no longer see
The vertical shafts of glass-stained sunlight
That dramatise our holiness.

Harbingers of death. We carefully avoid them
As we surge forward to answer the summons
Of church bells they no longer hear.

Chichén Itzá

Toltec temples ascend to gods guarding
The secrets of time.
What brave nation built so high above the jungle floor
To divide the years into precise segments,
And to appease the gods of their own imagination
With human sacrifice?
What splendour daubed this city and lit its walls with sound
As priests assumed the feathers of the Quetzal bird
(Extinct emblem of their fallen dynasty),
And donned the hideous death mask of the jaguar,
Stealing from the gods the panoply of power?

They assumed too much,
These human gods.
Some mightier force than they
Has let run the sands of time,
Wiped out the gaudy colours,
Muted the mysterious echoes,
And replaced them with a jungle growth of vines,
The vibrant hue of flowers
And brilliant flash of blue
That marks the mot-mot
Clock bird,
Sole tenant of the creviced stone,
Who idly beats his pendulous tail
In mockery
And wears a russet chest
As token of the blood
Sun-dried upon these altar stones
In Mayan Chichén Itzá,

Whose limestone pools
(Once filled with sacrificial bones)
Now cool the cohorts of a new invasion;
The turnstile tourist horde.

A Course Critique – for Mem Fox

'Look, Mem! Here's a word-stripped effing sonnet.'

'What a super opening, petal-face.
It's well-punctuated and, just in case
I doubted the time you spent upon it,
You sent me much more than just your sonnet.
You sent me a sheaf of blood-stained drafts. Ace!
Fantastic! I'm listening, petal-face.'

'Shit, Mem! She won't start. Help! Lift the bonnet.'

Fox knew Watt. Put a spanner in the works.
Cleaned out clichés. Ejected adjectives.
Stripped words from thoughts. Tightened oily phrases.

And then we conferenced. Ironed out the quirks
And gutted English stuffed with superlatives
And became free from our word-stuffed mazes.

To Jane Covernton (of Omnibus Books)

I composed a verse for *Putrid Poems*
Several weeks ago
And hid it
Because it was no good.

To my delight,
However,
I now find that it has decomposed.
The lines have crumbled
And the words have fallen apart
Leaving rotten little letters
All over my desk
Like d K.

This is what's left of it.

The Hare

At the edge of the trees
Shadows are strewn,
A motionless frieze
Etched by the moon.

An instinct of fear
Is caught in its light.
Its footfall like snowfall,
Soft in the night.

Migration

O Swallow, winging south with breathless pace,
Drawn once more to sun and sand-strewn reaches,
Teach me how to skim across those beaches
That long for shadow birds to fan their face
With movement. Take me to the market place
Where stone-faced orators in dark niches
Mock weathered women, whose stores of peaches
Are bartered with gold-gapped smiles wreathed in lace.

Restless, I yearn to leave this mud-built nest
To seek athirst each new-discovered thing,
Impelled upon a never-ending quest
For sweetness. I shall fly on ceaseless wing
And move from place to place as Nature's guest
Committed ever more to search and sing.

Wisdom

Wisdom's an essence to be distilled.
Too many words and the damned thing's killed.

Good and Evil

In the depths of my desire
Are two things
I can't quite grasp.
I know that I am human
So long as I keep reaching for them:
Good and Evil.
But always one stands in the way
When I grasp for the other.

Guilt

Bad memories escape from silent deeps
To don their haunting shape. They flood unbidden
Into my mind, whence they expose a midden
Heap of life consumed with pleasure. Shame creeps
Across the pile, destroying it. She leaps
Upon the back of a wild nightmare ridden
Through deep depravities no longer hidden,
And pierces my conscience with demented shrieks.

Nothing is in her taunts except my fear.
They goad me, goad me till I turn and flee
To seek another kindred soul to share
The night and soothe these dreams that trouble me.
But if I find you, kindred soul, beware!
Lest I spice your pleasures with Ecstasy.

Bees

The rising sap brought forth its crop of weeds
To mar the neat designs she'd planned at ease.
To combat them she sank upon her knees
To separate the sinners from the seeds
Of her imagined blossoming of needs.
So set was she upon necessities
She failed to see the swarm, the mass of bees,
Or hear their drone, discordant in the trees.

In wedlock too, self-chained upon a wheel
Of daily grind that will not let her free,
That slowly takes away her power to sing,
She trades the beauty of dreams for 'real'
She works as do the bees, and has their sting.
Life fast fades, yet she will not turn the key.

The Kangaroo

I turned from watering the compost heap
To see him grazing, a mere five paces
Behind me, nibbling on parsley laces
As tame, it seemed, as a domestic sheep
Then I saw the gash; his thigh torn deep.
He turned to me, but maintained his stasis
His limpid eye gazed, showing no traces
Of fear or pain. 'Tis only humans weep.

Twelve days he stayed. Nature herself did weave
His ragged wound. The shade of olive trees
Cooled him by day. The full moon sparked his eye
And gave him strength. We didn't see him leave.
We wished him well, but Nature was a tease.
For when the moon waned, he came back to die.

Why the Sonnet?

If I can remain within the sonnet
My feelings will be suitably constrained
And held in counterpoint to wit well trained
To smother emotion and stamp upon it.
Prolix emotion is a kind of vomit
Gushing unstemmed until the page is stained
With the sentimental trash we disdained
To read at school when we came upon it.

Some people expose themselves in free verse,
Others in rhyming couplets. Even worse
Are those who splash their thoughts in purple prose.
I fear, forsooth, there is no hope for those.
It's a matter of form. There is a code.
I'll stick with sonnets till I've mined the lode.

Ninja

Ninja, our daughter's cat, is Siamese.
When I start to write, he leaps upon my lap
Just as soon as he hears the keyboard's tap,
He purrs and rubs his chin against my knees.
If I don't stop, he walks upon the keys.
'I am your critic. What you write is pap!
'I need attention ere I take my nap.
'So, scratch behind the left ear if you please.'

He knows the most important time is now
And full attention to the one we love
Is vital to any relationship.
If I forget him, he lets forth a miaow
And if I multitask, he's not above
A nudge with his head or a gentle nip.

Lemons

Our lemon tree bears fruit throughout the year.
Its acid portioned out, it does suffice
To zest our daily gin, by slice and slice,
But in some seasons it does overbear
A windfall crop beyond our wildest fear
And we feel honour-bound to count the price
And squeeze the juice into small trays of ice
For use in times when lemons are too dear.

Apportioned piquancy can spice our life,
Add sharpened pleasure to our venal sin.
Too much doth mar and turn our pleasures sour.
We needs must store it to avoid such strife
And measure it in spirit, djinn by djinn,
Lest acid wit should sear and overpower.

Nightfall

Shall we be out there as the sun goes down,
Spreading his gold upon the dark grey sea;
As the moon spills light through the ghostly tree
And draws round her limbs a silvery gown
Of gossamer lacework leaves? When the crown
Of stars appears, will you be here to see
Orion hunt dreams wreathed in mystery?
Shall we ride with him to track our dream down?

Or shall we draw curtains across that dream,
And once more shun evening's golden light
To view by remote other people's plight,
Their drama, their lives played out on our screen?
Why choose the shadow when we could careen
Wild with the stars and fly brave through the night?

Remains

A pile of clothes lies in one corner
Of your erstwhile space;
A felt hat and scarf
against the cold
that now seeps through your bones
eternally
and my memory,
and my memories.

Notes

1. These poems were originally written to accompany photographs taken by my daughter in Yooren, a village in the Afar, a wild and remote region of northern Ethiopia.

2. The Afar region is the site of some of the earliest humanoid fossil discoveries and amongst the hottest and harshest inhabited regions on earth. The Afar people (Danakil) claim to be descended from Noah's son, Ham.

3. The nearest water source for the people of Yooren is from the Awash River, which lies about a kilometre from the community. Traditionally the women and young girls carry up to twenty to thirty litres of water on their backs in goatskins. This is a chore that takes place at least two to three times a day, even throughout a women's pregnancy. Maternal mortality and miscarriage rates are very high, and many of the women suffer from sciatica neuritis and lordosis (saddle-back), a pronounced curvature of the lumber spine.

4. According to Ethiopian medieval texts, the Ethiopian kings were descended from King Solomon and the Queen of Sheba (who is called Makeda in Ethiopia). They also claim that the Ark of the Covenant was secretly brought to Ethiopia by Solomon's son, Menelik, the first in a long line of kings of Ethiopia.

5. Trachoma, a disease eventually causing blindness, is borne by flies and it is said that 85% of the population of northern Ethiopia is affected. Treatment by health professionals involves access to water for face washing, use of a cheap antibiotic eye ointment or oral antibiotic tablets and simple surgery when the eyelids turn in.

6. *Jile*: the curved hunting knife of the Afar people of northern Ethiopia.

7. A 2012 World Economic Forum report projected that small-scale farming's contribution to global food production would fall from 40% in 2010 to zero by 2030 – being replaced by industrial large-scale mono-crop farming. Mono-cropping of sugar and coffee are two examples in Ethiopia of practices that cause chronic soil deterioration, water overuse and chemical pollution. Small-farm agriculture currently supplies about 70% of local food. As it disappears, I wonder who will produce food for small-scale markets and poor people around the world. These practices not only displace local food diversity but also erode ancient cultures in many ways far wiser than our own.

Remains

A pile of clothes lies in one corner
Of your erstwhile space;
A felt hat and scarf
against the cold
that now seeps through your bones
eternally
and my memory,
and my memories.

Notes

1. These poems were originally written to accompany photographs taken by my daughter in Yooren, a village in the Afar, a wild and remote region of northern Ethiopia.

2. The Afar region is the site of some of the earliest humanoid fossil discoveries and amongst the hottest and harshest inhabited regions on earth. The Afar people (Danakil) claim to be descended from Noah's son, Ham.

3. The nearest water source for the people of Yooren is from the Awash River, which lies about a kilometre from the community. Traditionally the women and young girls carry up to twenty to thirty litres of water on their backs in goatskins. This is a chore that takes place at least two to three times a day, even throughout a women's pregnancy. Maternal mortality and miscarriage rates are very high, and many of the women suffer from sciatica neuritis and lordosis (saddle-back), a pronounced curvature of the lumber spine.

4. According to Ethiopian medieval texts, the Ethiopian kings were descended from King Solomon and the Queen of Sheba (who is called Makeda in Ethiopia). They also claim that the Ark of the Covenant was secretly brought to Ethiopia by Solomon's son, Menelik, the first in a long line of kings of Ethiopia.

5. Trachoma, a disease eventually causing blindness, is borne by flies and it is said that 85% of the population of northern Ethiopia is affected. Treatment by health professionals involves access to water for face washing, use of a cheap antibiotic eye ointment or oral antibiotic tablets and simple surgery when the eyelids turn in.

6. *Jile*: the curved hunting knife of the Afar people of northern Ethiopia.

7. A 2012 World Economic Forum report projected that small-scale farming's contribution to global food production would fall from 40% in 2010 to zero by 2030 – being replaced by industrial large-scale mono-crop farming. Mono-cropping of sugar and coffee are two examples in Ethiopia of practices that cause chronic soil deterioration, water overuse and chemical pollution. Small-farm agriculture currently supplies about 70% of local food. As it disappears, I wonder who will produce food for small-scale markets and poor people around the world. These practices not only displace local food diversity but also erode ancient cultures in many ways far wiser than our own.

8. The Afar has fewer hospitals, schools or social services than almost any other region in Ethiopia. Children generally die young and about one-third of Afar children do not live beyond the age of five. According to the World Health Organisation (WHO), only about 5% of the Afar population has access to proper health care and there are only two hospitals that serve the entire region, which covers 278,000 square kilometres.

9. A child with an assault rifle such as the Soviet-made AK-47 is a fearsome match for anyone. These weapons are very simple to use. The AK-47 can be stripped and reassembled by a child of ten.

10. In the Afar region of Ethiopia, female genital cutting (FGC) is performed on almost every young girl, causing her to suffer multifaceted complications for the rest of her life. The maternal and infant morbidity and mortality is devastating, with each woman facing an exceptionally high risk of dying in childbirth.

11. The Afar (Danakil) Depression sits on a junction of tectonic plates where the Earth's crust is rifting apart at a rate of one or two centimetres per year. Earthquakes and a volcanic eruption in 2005 forced open a wide gap on the surface, known as the Dabbahu fissure.

12. There are arguments both for and against charcoal burning in Ethiopia. However, the recent escalation of unlicensed clear-fell logging to satisfy an ever-growing demand for fuel is unsustainable and responsible for further deforestation in a country that has already lost 97% of its trees.

13. Song of Solomon (7:4): 'Thy neck is as a tower of ivory; thine eyes like the fishpools in Heshbon, by the gate of Bath-rabbim.'

14. The pantoum is derived from a Malay verse form and has repeating lines throughout. The second and fourth lines of each stanza are repeated as the first and third lines of the next. Additionally, to complete the circularity, the third and first lines of the poem become, respectively, the second and fourth lines of the last stanza.

15. Howdah: the carriage on the back of the elephant in which tourists ride.

16. The elephant crush – a method by which wild elephants are tamed using restriction in a cage.

www.ingramcontent.com/pod-product-compliance
Lightning Source LLC
Chambersburg PA
CBHW070929080526
44589CB00013B/1451